Ready for Laughs!

A Treasury of Undersea Humor

Based on the TV series *SpongeBob SquarePants*®
created by Stephen Hillenburg as seen on Nickelodeon®

ISBN 0-439-62693-5

12 11 10 9 8 7 6 5 4 3 2 1   4 5 6 7 8 9/0

Printed in the U.S.A.

First Scholastic printing, March 2004

Ready for Laughs!

A Treasury of Undersea Humor

by David Lewman and David Fain

SCHOLASTIC INC.

New York   Toronto   London   Auckland   Sydney
Mexico City   New Delhi   Hong Kong   Buenos Aires

Table of Contents

Jokes

What does Patrick's best friend take before he goes to bed?

A sponge bath.

How did Squidward feel when he found an electric eel in his clarinet?

He was shocked.

Who's yellow and dances in an undersea barn?

SpongeBob SquareDance.

What does Patrick's best friend keep in his closet?
SpongeBob's spare pants.

What happened when SpongeBob played checkers against Squidward?
He beat him fair and square.

Why can you trust SpongeBob?
He always gives you a square deal.

What does SpongeBob eat
three times a day?
A square meal.

What's the secret to wearing clothes underwater?

You have to water your pants every day.

Which sea will make you go ape?

The Chimpansea.

Sandy: Knock, knock.

SpongeBob: Who's there?

Sandy: Sweat.

SpongeBob: Sweat who?

Sandy: 'S wet down here, isn't it?

Patrick: Why did the fish stay home from school?

Mrs. Puff: She was feeling a little under the water.

Squidward: Why does SpongeBob get in so much trouble?

Mr. Krabs: Because he's always in deep water.

Where does SpongeBob sleep?
In a water bed.

SpongeBob: Knock, knock.
Squidward: Who's there?
SpongeBob: Water.
Squidward: Water who?
SpongeBob: What're you doin',
Squidward?

SpongeBob: Were you a
happy baby, Patrick?
Patrick: Yes, because I
knew someday
I'd be a star.

Pearl: What kind of
star is Patrick?
Squidward: The kind
that's not very bright.

What do you get when you cross a squid and a pig?

An oinktopus.

What do you get
when you cross a
squid and a parrot?

A squawktopus.

Who robs banks
and shoots ink?
Billy the Squid.

Are shellfish warm?
No, they're clammy.

What would Sandy be if she got her picture in a magazine?

A cover squirrel.

What did SpongeBob say
after he fell in the dough?
"I'm bready!"

Who cleans the rooms at
Bikini Bottom's hotel?
Mer-maids.

What has a girl's head, a fish's
tail, and speaks very softly?
A murmurmaid.

What has a cat's head and
a fish's tail?

A purrmaid.

What has two seats,
and sticks to underwater
rocks?

A barnacle built for two.

What do his friends sing on SpongeBob's birthday?

"For he's a jolly good yellow!"

How does SpongeBob learn about new parts of the ocean?

He lets it all soak in.

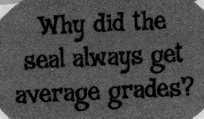

Why did the
seal always get
average grades?

He was
a C Lion.

What's big and gray and
lives underwater?
An eelephant.

How did Patrick do on his
bubble test?
He blew it.

Who's the best dressed creature in the ocean?

The swordfish—he always looks sharp!

What do you get when you cross a fish and a grizzly?
A bearacuda.

Which fish is the cheesiest?
The barragouda.

Which fish is the smelliest?

The stink ray.

Why did SpongeBob chase the stinging fish?

He wanted to catch some rays.

Why did the stingray
speak to the diver?
He wanted to have
a manta-man talk.

Why did the scary fish
always swim by himself?
He wanted to be a lone shark.

What do you get when you
cross a shellfish and a rabbit?
The Oyster Bunny.

What do you get when
you cross a scary fish
with an anteater?
An aardshark.

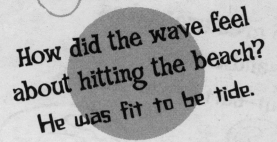

How did the wave feel
about hitting the beach?
He was fit to be tide.

Who got to the
beach first, the
big wave or the
little wave?
In the end, they
were tide.

Which sea creature makes the best sandwiches?
The peanut-butter-and-jellyfish.

Where do fish like to go on vacation?
Finland.

Which book is every fish's favorite?
Huckleberry Fin.

Which whale is
the saddest?
The blue whale.

What will happen to Plankton if
he breaks the law?
He'll be thrown
in whale.

Why does Patrick think octopuses are sweet? He heard they're covered with suckers.

What do you call an underwater sheep? A scubaaaaaa diver.

How did Sandy feel when she first reached Bikini Bottom? She was floored.

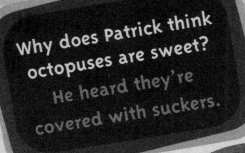

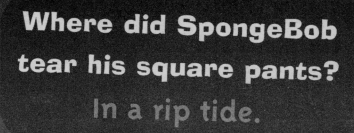

Where did SpongeBob tear his square pants?

In a rip tide.

What's every porpoise's favorite musical?

Guys and Dolphins.

SpongeBob:
Knock, knock.

Squidward:
Who's there?

SpongeBob:
Conch.

Squidward:
Conch who?

SpongeBob:
Conch you open
this door?

What do you use to catch starfish?

A film reel.

What do you use to
catch electric eels?

A lightning rod.

Why did the fisherman
keep catching drapes?

He was using a curtain rod.

Why did the ocean flood the stadium?
It was doing the wave!

Why did Plankton
punch the sand?
He wanted to hit
the beach.

What does SpongeBob
use to write home
from the beach?
Sandpaper.

SpongeBob and Patrick: Knock, knock.

Squidward: Who's there?

SpongeBob and Patrick: Seaweed.

Squidward: Seaweed who?

SpongeBob and Patrick: See, we'd come in if you'd open the door.

**Where did the seaweed
find a job?
In the
"Kelp Wanted" ads.**

Why did SpongeBob salute his boss?
He wanted to hail a crab.

How did the jury find the fish?
Gill-ty.

What happened when
SpongeBob rode on his pet snail?
He got Gary-ied away.

What's Gary like first
thing in the morning?
A little sluggish.

Which fish is
the funniest?
The cartoona.

What game do fish
love to play?

Salmon Says.

How did SpongeBob get across the beach so quickly?

He took a shore-cut.

How do you stop a fish stampede?

Head 'em off at the bass.

SpongeBob and Patrick: Knock, knock.

Squidward: Who's there?

SpongeBob and Patrick: Porous.

Squidward: Porous who?

SpongeBob and Patrick: Pour us something to drink—we're thirsty!

When SpongeBob's neighbor talks, what comes out of his mouth?

Squid words.

What does Patrick listen to in his home?

Rock music.

What do you use to cut the ocean?

A seasaw.

What do you get when you cross an ape and a crustacean?

A shrimpanzee.

Why did the coral stand on his head? He wanted to turn over a new reef.

Why don't little fish sleep at night? They're afraid of the shark.

Which squid is the friendliest?
The cuddlefish.

Why did the cantaloupe
jump in the ocean?
It wanted to be a
watermelon.

When is SpongeBob like a bell?
When he's wrung out.

What did the patty
do when it saw
SpongeBob's new
spatula?
It flipped.

SpongeBob: Can't you say anything nice about Patrick?

Squidward: He has his points.

Which part of a boat is the grouchiest?
The stern.

Which part of a boat is the most polite?
The bow.

How do you catch cyberfish?
With an *Internet*.

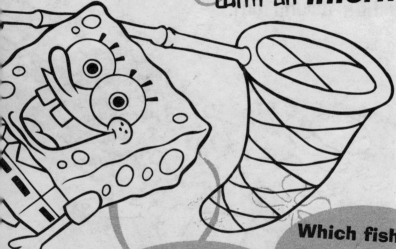

Which fish hates to be alone?
The grouper.

Which fish can slide across ice?
The skate.

SpongeBob: Knock, knock.

Squidward: Who's there?

SpongeBob: Saul.

Squidward: Saul who?

SpongeBob: Saltwater's the best—got any?

What happened when SpongeBob invited too many people onto his boat?
He went a little overboard.

Why did the ocean take the afternoon off?
He wanted to play gulf.

Which fish finds the best bargains?
The sale-fish

Avast there, mateys! Here's the rarest sea creature of them all—SpongeBob SquarePants! He may look like an ordinary sponge to you landlubbers, but take my word for it, he's the most unique talking yellow cube filled with holes you'll ever find on the ocean floor—or any floor for that matter.

I'M READY

Hi! I'm SpongeBob SquarePants! And I'm ready to start another wonderful day here in Bikini Bottom. I'm ready, I'm ready, I'm ready! Whoops! Look at the time! I still have to do my morning workout, eat a healthy breakfast of Kelpo, and feed my pet snail, Gary, before I go to work.

FRIENDS and NEIGHBORS

I've got lots of neat friends. Let me introduce you to some of them.

Patrick is my best friend. We do everything together: jellyfishing, blowing bubbles, playing superheroes, hunting for pirate treasure, you name it. He also likes sleeping, drooling, and lying dormant under his rock.

Sandy is a land squirrel, which means she has to wear a hat full of air and a pressure suit to live underwater. She's a great surfer and an excellent karate expert, just like me! She's from this faraway place called Texas. That's why she talks the way she does. Don't worry, you get used to it after a while.

That's my next door neighbor, Squidward Tentacles. Even though we work all day together at the Krusty Krab, I never get tired of spending time with him. He practices his clarinet a lot, although he never seems to get any better. He doesn't have time to play with Patrick and me. We practically have to drag him out of his house kicking and screaming just to get him to have some fun.

Mr. Krabs is my boss, and the owner of the Krusty Krab restaurant where Squidward and I work. People say he's cheap, but I consider it an honor to work for the creator of the Krabby Patty! Sometimes I think that maybe I should be paying him!

AROUND BIKINI BOTTOM

Patrick's rock

two-story pineapple

Easter Island head

Here's where we live. The two-story pineapple is mine. It's fully equipped with a shellphone, state of the art stuffed animal barbells, and a foghorn alarm clock. Next door is my pal Squidward's Easter Island head, and next to that is my friend Patrick's rock. Every weekend I use my reef blower to keep my yard seashell free and sparkling.

Howdy, y'all! This is my house, the treedome! It's full of the driest, purest, airyest air in the whole sea! I have all the comforts of home: an exercise wheel, a picnic table, an oak tree, and a trampoline. The treedome is made of polyurethane (that's a fancy name for plastic).

Ahoy, mateys! An anchor is what me and me daughter, Pearl, call home! My darlin' Pearl is pretty hard to miss, and a pretty miss ta boot! Har! Har!

Daddy, you're embarrassing me! I'm going to cheerleading practice!

She's a whale y'see (takes after her mother that way).

BORN to COOK

Here it is, my work place, the finest eating establishment ever established for eating— the Krusty Krab! Home of that tasty, juicy, scrumptious, warm mouthful of steamy goodness called the Krabby Patty! Would you like fries with that?

Across the street is the Chum Bucket, owned by Mr. Krabs's archrival, Plankton! With the help of his computer, Karen, Plankton's always trying to steal the Krabby Patty recipe. People say he's evil, but I think he just needs a friend.

It's not that easy to become a member of the Krusty crew. You really need the expertise to properly prepare the perfect Krabby Patty.

First comes the bun, then the patty, followed by ketchup, mustard, pickles, onions, lettuce, cheese, tomatoes and bun— in that order.

THE RENAISSANCE CEPHALOPOD

Hello, friends, and welcome to my private art gallery. I have conquered all artistic mediums in my pursuit of the perfect self-portrait. Being the only squid of culture in this backward community is a heavy burden, but one I could gladly bear if it weren't for the constant pestering of . . . SPONGEBOB SQUAREPANTS! I can't get a moment's peace from that nuisance and his equally annoying friend Patrick!

Do you know they come over every day (and twice on Sundays) to ask me if I want to go jellyfishing? Jellyfishing? Me? Have you ever heard of anything so ridiculous?!

And that's just the beginning! SpongeBob throws me birthday parties when it's not my birthday,

he's always making a racket,

and as if that isn't bad enough, he keeps leaving his undergarments on my front lawn!

BUBBLE-BLOWING TECHNIQUE

Wanna blow some bubbles? It only costs twenty-five cents. Here's your bubble wand, dipped and ready to go. Remember, it's all in the technique!

* First, go like this.
* Spin around—stop!
* Double-take three times
  . . . one, two, and three.
* Pelvic Thrust—Woo Hoo!
* Stomp on your right foot.
  (Don't forget it!)
* Now it's time to bring it
  around town. Bring it
  around town!
* Then you do this, then
  this, and this and that and
  thisandthatandthisandthat!

You can blow bubbles in all sorts of interesting shapes.
Try some of these:

A CUBE

DUCKS

A DANCE PARTNER

A CENTIPEDE

A TUGBOAT

A BUTTERFLY

AN ELEPHANT

You can also whisper messages inside the bubbles to send to your friends. Just be sure the right person gets the right message. Or that the message is from the right person. Or that the message goes to the person on your right. Or that you don't forget . . . oh, tartar sauce! I forgot who I was sending this message to!

CHAMPIONS
of the DEEP

You're just in time for my favorite television show:
The Adventures of MermaidMan! I've got a genuine
imitation copy of his uniform. Patrick says his young
ward, Barnacle Boy, is better, but that's just because
that's who he is when we play superheroes.

They are so cool!
Patrick and I found
out that MermaidMan and
Barnacle Boy live over at the
Shady Shoals older citizens' home.
We think they're working undercover!

Recently roused from retirement, the aquatic avengers have launched a new series of adventures, though now much older (and considerably less wiser). Watch in awe as they:

CHANGE A LIGHTBULB!

WAIT FOR THE AQUAPHONE REPAIRMAN!

EAT THEIR MEATLOAF!

ADJUST THEIR HEARING AIDS!

PLAY CHECKERS!

TRY TO REMEMBER WHERE THEY PARKED THE INVISIBLE BOATMOBILE!

BOATING SCHOOL QUIZ

When I'm not working, I go to Mrs. Puff's Boating School. I can hardly wait until I get my license. If only I didn't always get so nervous during the driving exam. Oh well, you know what they say—thirty-eighth time's the charm! (Okay, thirty-ninth!)

Mrs. Puff is the best boating teacher I've ever had. Well, actually she's the only boating teacher I've ever had. She's a puffer fish (which means she has her own built in airbag, which comes in very handy during those driving tests). Let's see how much you know about boating:

1 The front of the boat is called the
a) bow.
b) porthole.
c) stern.

2 The first thing you do when you're about to start the driving test is
a) floor it!
b) put it in drive.
c) start the boat.

3 Red means
a) floor it!
b) stop.
c) make a right turn.

4 If you see a big anchor in the middle of the road, you should
a) floor it!
b) crash into it.
c) jump over it.

5 The second thing you do when you're taking the driving test is
a) pop a wheelie.
b) put it in drive.
c) cross the finish line.

6 If you see someone in the crosswalk while you're driving, you should
a) get out and help him or her cross the street.
b) turn around and go the other way.
c) go upside down.

7 In boating terms, right is
a) starboard.
b) port.
c) wrong.

8 If your boat has a kitchen onboard it's called
a) the keel.
b) the hall monitor.
c) the galley.

9 If you have a walkie-talkie inside your head and someone else is telling you what to do during the driving test, you are
a) lucky.
b) dreaming.
c) cheating.

10 The last thing you should do when you're taking the driving test is
a) watch Mrs. Puff being taken away in an ambulance.
b) cross the finish line.
c) floor it!

SQUIDWARD SEZ

Our pal Squidward is always claiming that he doesn't want to play with SpongeBob and me. We know he's just playing a game where he says the opposite of what he really means (just like on Opposite Day). Let me show you. First he'll talk, and then I'll translate.

WHEN SQUIDWARD SAYS:

"How did I ever get surrounded by such loser neighbors?"

HE REALLY MEANS:

"I have the best neighbors in the world!"

WHEN SQUIDWARD SAYS:

"You're killing me, SpongeBob ... you really are!"

HE REALLY MEANS:

"Do it again!"

WHEN SQUIDWARD SAYS:

"Can we lower the volume, please?"

HE REALLY MEANS:

"Do it again . . . louder!"

WHEN SQUIDWARD SAYS:

"Oh, puh-leez!"

HE REALLY MEANS:

"You're welcome."

WHO SAID IT?

Hear me, surface dwellers! That simpleton starfish isn't the only one around here who knows something about language! I have created a foolproof device that allows me to perfectly imitate the voice of any resident of Bikini Bottom I choose! Don't ask how this will help me to obtain a Krabby Patty—it's far too complicated to explain to your miniscule mentalities. What I need from you is help in sorting out who says what! Match each sentence to the person most likely to have said it, and I may spare you when I destroy this miserable town!

1 "Mother O' Pearl!"

A SpongeBob

2 "Sea creatures assemble!"

B Patrick

3 "Is it already time to ruin Squid's day?"

C Sandy

4 "Meow."

D Squidward

5 "Ain't that just the bee's knees?"

E Mr. Krabs

6 "You guys want to lift some weights?"

F MermaidMan

7 "I'm ready!"

G Gary

8 "Oh, my aching tentacles!"

H Larry the Lobster

9 "Daddy, you're embarrassing me!"

I Mrs. Puff

10 "Whose turn is it to be hall monitor?"

J Pearl

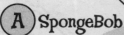

MUSSEL BEACH PARTY

This is Mussel Beach, where my friends and I sometimes go to have fun. Everyone has their own favorite things to do here, and at the nearby, wonderful, stinky mud puddle we call Goo Lagoon. I'll let them tell you themselves!

Well, I get really stoked from catching a wave! That's surfing, for all you nonaquatic wannabes. My favorite move is to do a handstand while shooting the tube. That way I can hang ten . . . fingers that is! I also enjoy playing Frisbee with my friends, although SpongeBob tends to try catching it with his face!

What I like doing at Goo Lagoon is lying on the sand and sleeping. Actually I like lying on the sand and sleeping anywhere. I don't even have to be on sand ... or even lying down. I just ... like ... zzz zzz zzz.

Well, if I wasn't always being bothered by certain very annoying people, I would luxuriate in working on my tan at Mussel Beach.

As for me, I like hanging out in the juice bar, singing beach music, and playing in the sand. But here are a few activities you want to avoid if you don't want to end up the biggest loser on the beach:

- Getting sand in your buns
- Forgetting your sunscreen (and getting sunburned)
- Being buried in the sand and getting left behind
- Ripping your pants (repeatedly)
- Pretending to drown

MAY I TAKE YOUR ORDER

THE KRUSTY KRAB, HOME OF THE ONE AND ONLY KRABBY PATTY!

Remember, at the Krusty Krab,

YOU ARE THE CAPTAIN!

SANDWICHES

$2.00

KRABBY PATTY

$2.50

DOUBLE KRABBY PATTY
WITH THE WORKS

KRUSTY COMBO KRABBY PATTY, FRIES, AND MEDIUM DRINK

$3.99

$3.00

KRUSTY DELUXE
DOUBLE KRABBY PATTY
WITH THE WORKS AND OYSTER SKINS

CRYING JOHNNIE
$2.25
KRABBY PATTY
WITH EXTRA ONIONS

$1.99
BUBBLE BASS SPECIAL
KRABBY PATTY HOLD THE PICKLES
(UNDER YOUR TONGUE)

$1.75
MINNOW MEAL
SEANUT BUTTER AND JELLYFISH JELLY
SANDWICH, FRIES, AND SMALL DRINK

SIDES

OYSTER SKINS . . . . $.50
FRIES $1.25
SEAWEED SALAD $1.50
CORAL BITS $1.95

DRINKS

SALTY SHAKES **$.99**

DR. KELP OR
DIET DR. KELP **$.89**

And don't forget, every Tuesday is Mouthful of Clams
Day! Everyone who shows up with a mouthful of
clams gets a free drink!

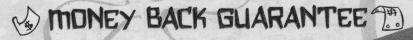

MONEY BACK GUARANTEE

THE SECRETS to SUCCESSFUL JELLYFISHING

Welcome to Jellyfish Fields, where wild jellyfish roam, just waiting to be captured. This is the best place in Bikini Bottom to go jellyfishing. Here are a few pointers for you beginners:

⊙ Bring a good solid net. Be sure to name it. Mine's called "Ol' Reliable."

⊙ Remember, SAFETY FIRST! Always wear your safety glasses.

⊙ Firmly grasp the net.

⊙ Always set the jellyfish free after you've caught it (you wouldn't like being kept in a jar either).

⊙ It helps if you sing "La, la, la" or "Da, da, da, da dum" while you jellyfish.

⊙ Disguise yourself as a piece of coral in order to get close to your prey.

⊙ Watch out for those stingers!

The jellyfish who live in Bikini Bottom are completely different from all other jellyfish in the sea. For example, they make a loud buzzing sound when they swim, they live in hives, and produce a delicious strawberry-flavored jelly. There's nothing like the taste of natural jelly from a jellyfish.

Remember, these jellyfish aren't pets, they're wild animals. They have powerful electrical stingers and use them when angry. They love to dance, and can't resist a good solid beat. But be warned: they don't like clarinet music (at least they don't like the way Squidward plays clarinet music)!

SPONGEBOB'S BUSY SCHEDULE

Sometimes I have so much to do it's hard to keep it straight. I'm glad I've got someplace to write it all down!

Monday — 11

Boating Exam today— don't forget to bring apple for Mrs. Puff. (Some bandages might not be a bad idea either.)

Sunday — 10

Opposite Day. Be sure to act like Squidward.

Friday — 15

15th of the month . . . Annoy Squidward Day! Call Patrick.

Saturday — 16

Squidward's Birthday!

Sunday — 17

Annual Jellyfish Convention in Ukulele Bottom. Find snail-sitter for Gary.

Tuesday 19

Have Squidward cover as fry cook. Make sure Krusty Krab is well-stocked with antacid tablets before leaving. Buy Mr. Krabs a gift to make up for loss in profits.

Wednesday 20

Squidward's Birthday!

Thursday 21

Glove World Grand Opening! Remind Patrick we need to stand in line all weekend to be sure we are the very first ones inside, just like last year.

Saturday 23

Sign Up Deadline for Mussel Beach Anchor Throw. Make sure to keep Sandy occupied and far away from Goo Lagoon. Prepare karate ambush?

Sunday 24

Squidward's Birthday!

Tuesday 26

Employee of the Month Judging Begins. Break Squidward's alarm clock.

Wednesday 27

Anniversary of first Day met Sandy. Definitely prepare Karate ambush! Pay day. Buy Mr. Krabs a sympathy card.

Friday 29

Squidward's Birthday!

SNAIL CARE

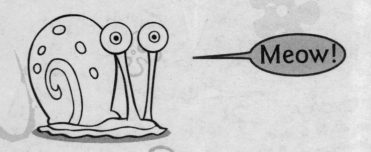

Meow!

Okay, I'll tell them, Gary. Gary wants me to let you know the most important information in the care and feeding of pet snails:

1. Snails need lots of food. They get one can of snail food in the morning and one can at night.

2. Don't let them get salty. Make sure they have plenty of water.

3. They need to be walked twice a day.

4. Snails love to play "fetch." Bring something to read, this can take awhile.

5. Your pet snail's "meowing" at the moon can annoy the neighbors. Try to keep it to a minimum.

6. Snails are natural-born poets. Encourage their artistic expression.

7. VERY, VERY IMPORTANT: Whatever you do, don't let yourself get accidentally injected with snail plasma.

DANGERS of the DEPTHS

Howdy, y'all. As Bikini Bottom's resident science expert, I'm here to tell y'all about a few sea critters you should give a wide berth to should they ever cross yer path:

Giant Clam. I tussled with one of these rascals myself the first time SpongeBob and I met. They're just big bullies. A few well-placed karate chops will more'n likely send them on their way with their tails betwixt their legs (if'n they had any legs, that is).

Nematodes (or undersea worms). These hungry little dudes don't look like much, but put a passel of them together and they can gnaw a coral reef down to a stub in ten seconds flat.

The Mother of All Jellyfish. This is the large economy-sized version of those cute little fellers who float out in Jellyfish Fields. But this mamma packs quite a wallop when it comes to stingers. Just ask Squidward.

Anchovies. Just like nematodes these little dudes ain't anything to be afraid of in small numbers, but fill a few tour buses with schools of these hungry fish, and they're as likely to stampede as look at ya! And to top it off, they're smellier than all get out.

Poison Sea Urchins. They're tiny and spiny and make you itch all over.

The Flying Dutchman. Although technically not a critter, he's more of a bogeyman ghost-type varmint. Anyhoo, he's as ornery as Mr. Krabs on payday and twice as ugly, so keep yer distance or he'll steal yer soul!

DID YOU KNOW?

Did you know that in Bikini Bottom—

Moss always points to civilization.

Through the misuse of time travel, Squidward invented the art of jellyfishing.

The specialty of the house at Plankton's restaurant, The Chum Bucket, is Chumbalaya. (No wonder he doesn't have any customers!)

SpongeBob has won the employee of the month award twenty-six months in a row.

The Flying Dutchman haunts the Seven Seas because he was never put to rest (people used his body for a window display after he died).

✽ In the future, everything will be chrome and there will be 486 letters in the alphabet (one for each SpongeTron clone produced).

☺ **Patrick knows a lot about head injuries.**

✽ Mr. Krabs has an acute sense of smell.

☺ **SpongeBob has had the following items inside his head:**

-A towel   -Plankton

-A walkie-talkie   -A lightbulb
                    (He makes a pretty good disco ball.)

✽ Squidward has a lifetime subscription to *Frown Digest Magazine*.

☺ Souls look like pickles.

✽ SpongeBob also plays a mean conch.

Did y'all know that up in
the surface world . . .

✳ SpongeBob SquarePants series
creator Stephen Hillenburg has a
degree in marine biology as well as
experimental animation.

☺ SpongeBob was originally
named SpongeBoy, but someone
was already using that name, so
the "y" became a "b."

✻ **Ernest Borgnine** and **Tim Conway** provide the voices for MermaidMan and Barnacle Boy. This is the first time the two have worked together since *McHale's Navy*.

Staff writer **Mr. Lawrence** contributes spoken as well as written words for the series. He performs the voice of Mr. Krabs's archrival Plankton, the announcer at sporting events in Goo Lagoon, and several others. (He's also the voice of Philbert the turtle on *Rocko's Modern Life*).

✻ Painty the Pirate (seen at the beginning of each SpongeBob SquarePants episode singing the theme song) has the live-action lips of series creator **Stephen Hillenburg**.

What would you call Gary if he lived on a farm?

"The Farmer in the Shell."

What's SpongeBob's favorite kind of knot?

The square knot.

What kind of shoes does SpongeBob wear?

Penny loofahs.

Was Squidward mad when
SpongeBob jumped on his mop?

Yes, he flew off the handle.

Why couldn't Plankton pay
for his Krabby Patty?

He was a little short.

What side order does Sandy always get with her Krabby Patty?

Squirrelly fries.

What does SpongeBob do when Squidward drops food?

He goes on a mopping spree!

What does Mr. Krabs like best about SpongeBob?

His buck teeth.

How does Mr. Krabs start every bedtime story?

"Once upon a dime . . ."

What's Mr. Krabs's favorite kind of bread?

Pumper-nickel.

What kind of nuts does Mr. Krabs like the best?

Cash-ews.

What do you see when Mr. Krabs's daughter smiles?

Her Pearly whites.

Why did SpongeBob fail his boating test?

He forgot to fasten his sea belt.

Mrs. Puff: Knock-knock.
SpongeBob: Who's there?
Mrs. Puff: Teach.
SpongeBob: Teach who?
Mrs. Puff: Teach yourself
        to drive—I give up!

RULES of the ROAD

What does every restaurant get when SpongeBob's behind the wheel?

A drive-through.

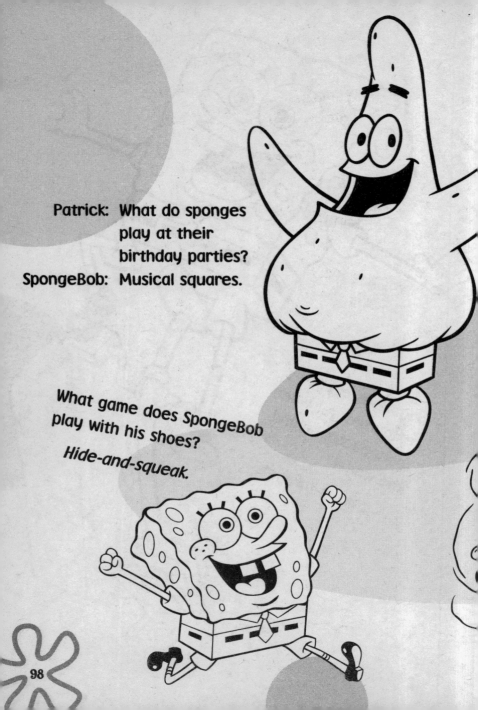

Patrick: What do sponges
play at their
birthday parties?
SpongeBob: Musical squares.

What game does SpongeBob
play with his shoes?
Hide-and-squeak.

98

Why did SpongeBob tear himself in half at the end of the party?

Because Sandy said it was time to split.

Why did SpongeBob wash the reef?

He was practicing good coral hygiene.

Is Plankton nice to
the reefs around
Bikini Bottom?

*No, he's rotten to
the coral.*

How do angelfish greet each other?

"Halo!"

Why does Sandy's fur stand
up on end whenever
Plankton's around?

*He rubs her the
wrong way.*

Where do Sandy and SpongeBob
practice their karate?

In choppy water.

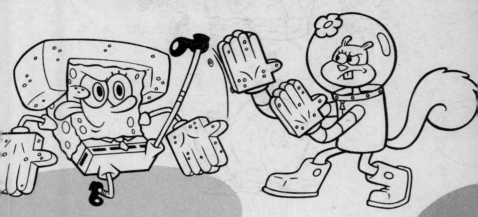

Sandy: What kind of pizza do
they serve at the
bottom of the ocean?
SpongeBob: Deep dish.

What kind of earrings does
Sandy's mom wear?

Mother-of-squirrel.

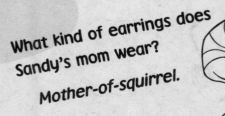

What do you get when you cross a squid and a dog?

An octo-pooch.

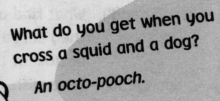

What do you get when
you cross a hunting dog,
a seagull, and a bumblebee?

A *bee-gull.*

Why can't Sandy play on Patrick's basketball team?

Because he's on an all-star team.

Why did Patrick stare at a mirror with his mouth open?

Squidward told him to watch his tongue.

What's salty and feels
good on a sunburn?

The Pacific Lotion.

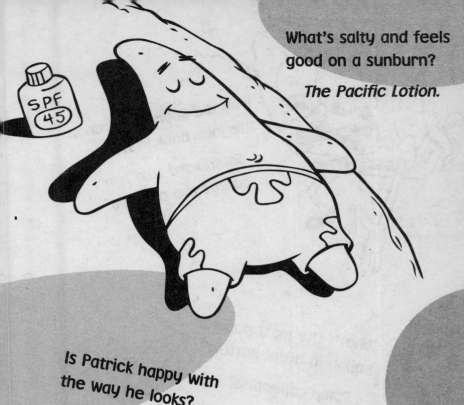

Is Patrick happy with
the way he looks?

Yes, he's tickled pink!

What makes Patrick grouchy?

Waking up on the wrong
side of the rock.

Why did SpongeBob chop the joke book in half?

Squidward told him to cut the comedy.

What's the most popular hobby in Bikini Bottom?

Damp collecting!

How did Squidward do in the hundred-yard dash?

He won by a nose.

What kind of ocean bird can't fly, can't swim, and can't catch fish?

A peli-can't.

What did SpongeBob yell when he dressed up as a bear?

"I'm Teddy!"

Squidward: Why does Gary meow?

SpongeBob: Because he doesn't know how to bark!

Patrick: Can you catch
a jellyfish with
a horn?
SpongeBob: Sure, if it's
a clari-net.

Patrick: Can you catch
a jellyfish with
a puppet?
SpongeBob: Sure, if it's
a mario-net.

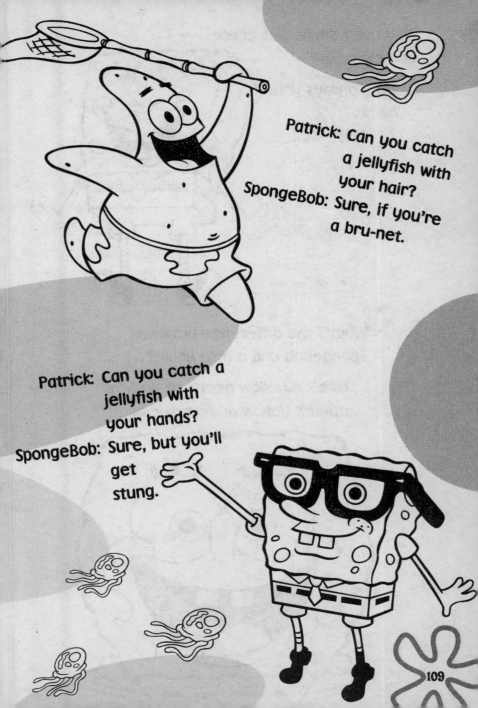

Patrick: Can you catch
a jellyfish with
your hair?
SpongeBob: Sure, if you're
a bru-net.

Patrick: Can you catch a
jellyfish with
your hands?
SpongeBob: Sure, but you'll
get
stung.

Why can't seahorses agree
on new rules?

*They always vote
neigh.*

What's the difference between
SpongeBob and a gold chain?

*One's a yellow necklace, and the
other's yellow and neck-less.*

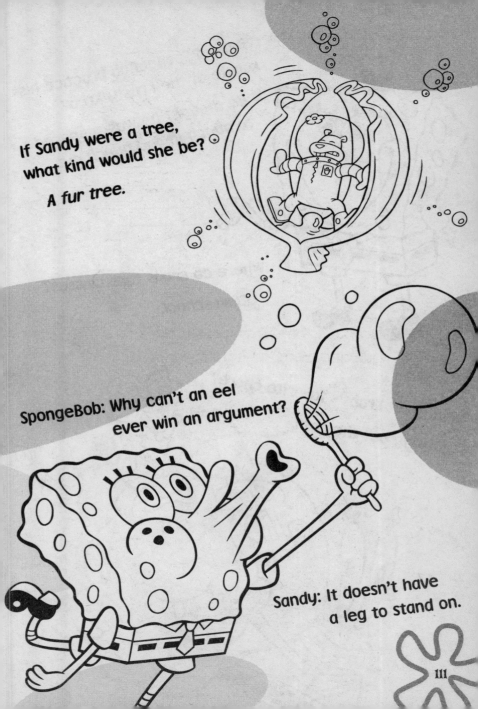

If Sandy were a tree, what kind would she be?

A fur tree.

SpongeBob: Why can't an eel ever win an argument?

Sandy: It doesn't have a leg to stand on.

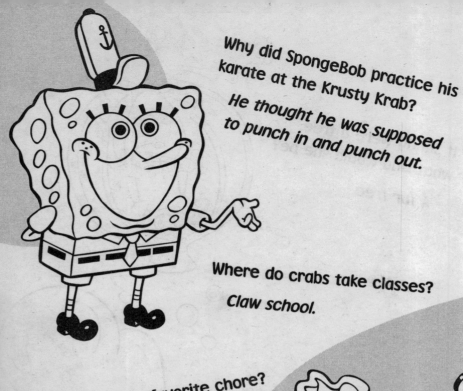

Why did SpongeBob practice his karate at the Krusty Krab?

He thought he was supposed to punch in and punch out.

Where do crabs take classes?

Claw school.

What's Mr. Krabs's favorite chore?

Taking out the cash.

Does SpongeBob have a good time at work?

Yes, he's the life of the patty.

What do Krabby Patties and long hair have in common?

They both fit in a bun.

Patrick: What do jellyfish
eat for breakfast?
SpongeBob: Floatmeal!

SpongeBob: What has two big
claws and is very
messy?
Patrick: A slobster!

114

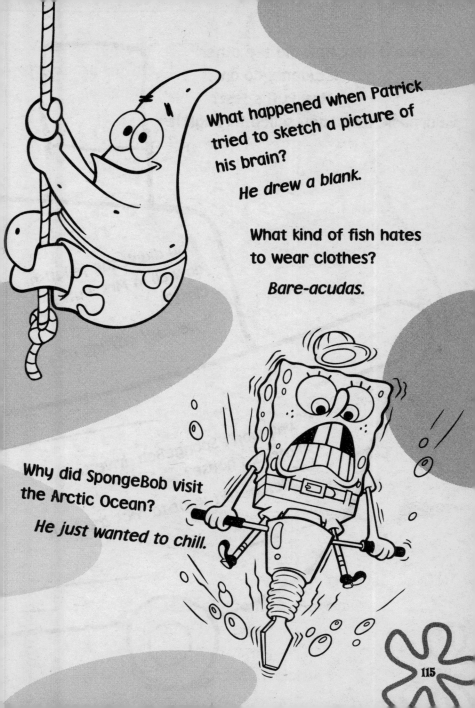

What happened when Patrick tried to sketch a picture of his brain?

He drew a blank.

What kind of fish hates to wear clothes?

Bare-acudas.

Why did SpongeBob visit the Arctic Ocean?

He just wanted to chill.

Mermaid Man: How did the other
students do on
Mrs. Puff's test?
Barnacle Boy: They sailed through it.

Why didn't the jellyfish
do well in Mrs. Puff's
class?

He kept drifting off.

Why won't SpongeBob drive to
Patrick's house?

He doesn't want to rock the boat.

What happened when SpongeBob ate mashed potatoes in Mrs. Puff's class?

He got a lump in his boat.

Patrick: Do you like barnacles?
SpongeBob: They're growing on me.

What did Mrs. Puff do at the end of SpongeBob's lesson?

She went on a long inflation.

Patrick: What's Plankton's favorite dessert?
SpongeBob: Shortcake.

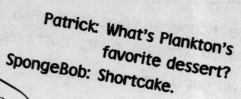

If Patrick's best friend were a dessert, what kind would he be?

Sponge cake.

Why would Mr. Krabs like to be a bowl of chocolate ice cream?

Because it's very rich.

Patrick: Who haunts the seven
seas but never vacuums?

SpongeBob: The Flying Dustman!

Mermaid Man: What does it take
to get into a fish choir?

Barnacle Boy: You have to be able
to carry a tuna.

Why did Patrick pull the
ship with a rope?

*He'd heard it was
a tugboat.*

Where would SpongeBob live
after an earthquake?

In a pineapple upside-down
house.

What do you call someone who
just sits around blowing into a
shell?

A conch potato!

Why didn't SpongeBob's pants
fall down during the hurricane?

He was saved by the belt.

Sandy: Why didn't the boy
penguin ask the girl
penguin out on a date?

SpongeBob: He got cold feet.

How is Sandy able to get around
Bikini Bottom without getting wet?

She has her dry-fur's license.

Why did the police
arrest Gary?

He was found at the
scene of the slime.

Knock-knock.
Who's there?
Hatch.
Hatch who?
Gesundheit!

Squidward: Knock-knock.
SpongeBob: Who's there?
Squidward: Claire.
SpongeBob: Claire who?
Squidward: Clarinets sound
beautiful,
don't they?

Why does Mr. Krabs have so many clocks in his house?

Because time is money.

Why does Mr. Krabs like to mop up?

Because inside every bucket, there's a buck.

Why did SpongeBob put his ear to the cash register?

Because Mr. Krabs told him, "Money talks."

Was Mr. Krabs mad when SpongeBob dropped the butter?

No, he let it slide.

What do you call Mr. Krabs when he's holding a coin?

A penny-pincher.

How does SpongeBob get exercise?

He does deep-sea bends.

Why did the quilt refuse to go to Bikini Bottom?

She didn't want to be a wet blanket.

What does SpongeBob
sleep in?

His under-square.

Where do sea cows
sleep at night?

In the barn-acle.

Squidward: Why do starfish get up
in the middle of the night?

SpongeBob: They have to twinkle.

How do you save jellyfish from drowning?

Throw them some life preserves.

Why couldn't Patrick understand what the jellyfish was saying?

It was way over his head.

Why did SpongeBob toss the sandwich at Patrick?

He wanted to throw him a surprise patty.

SpongeBob: What has horns, four legs,
and is made out of soap?
Sandy: A bubbalo!

When is SpongeBob like a battery?

When he gets all charged up!

Why doesn't SpongeBob
go to the barber?

He doesn't like to cut
corners.

Why do SpongeBob and Sandy
surf so well together?

They're on the same
wavelength.

What did Sandy say when she
finished gathering acorns?

"That's all, oaks!"

How does Sandy feel
about SpongeBob?

She's nuts about him!

What's SpongeBob's favorite
last-minute Halloween costume?

Swiss cheese.

Krusty Krab Gags

Why did the Krabby Patty go to the gym?

It wanted better buns.

How can you tell Krabby Patties come from the bottom of the ocean?

They're deep-fried.

Patrick: What do you give someone who turns a year older?

SpongeBob: A birthday patty!

Eat, Drink and Be Gary!

GARV

How does Gary get to the beach?
He takes the shell-evator.

Why did Gary go to Hollywood?

To be in slow business.

How do you clean Gary?

With snail polish.

What did Gary say when he hurt himself?

Me-OW!

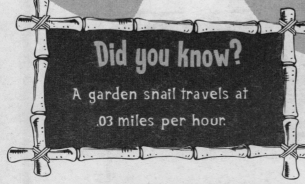

Did you know?

A garden snail travels at .03 miles per hour.

Just Squidding

Where does Squidward
sleep when he camps?

Z-Z-Z

In a tentacle.

What is Squidward's
favorite girl's name?

Clara Nett

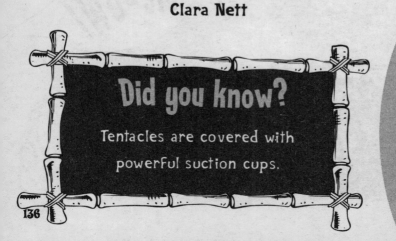

Did you know?

Tentacles are covered with
powerful suction cups.

How is Squidward like a tennis instructor?

They both know how to raise a racket.

Squidward: What's the best day for a Krabby Patty?

SpongeBob: Fry day!

She's Nutty!

How is SpongeBob's
favorite squirrel
like the beach?

Both are Sandy

What does
SpongeBob say
to cheer on Sandy?

"You go, squirrel!"

What does Sandy
read in school?

Tex books.

What's Sandy's Favorite ballet?

The Nutcracker.

A Whale of a Girl

Why did Pearl slap
the river?

Because it was freshwater.

How does Pearl
like her steak
cooked?

Whale done.

Why does Pearl like the ocean?

She's buoy crazy!

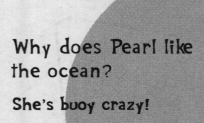

What did one whale say to the other whale?

"Say it, don't spray it!"

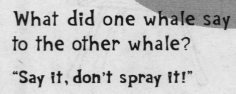

What's Pearl's favorite country?

Wales.

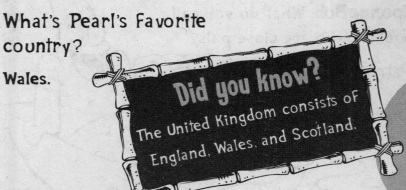

Did you know?
The United Kingdom consists of England, Wales, and Scotland.

Baby, I'm a Star(fish)!

Why did Patrick put on another jacket while he was painting?

The can said to add two coats.

SpongeBob: What do you call bubbles who are close pals?

Patrick: Best suds.

What do you get when you cross
Patrick with a cowboy?

A shooting star.

Why did Patrick bury his boom box?

Because the batteries were dead!

The End.